SPONSORED MORE DOWNLINES

How To Survive And Become Successful

By Using Best Kept Secret Strategy of Internet Network Marketing Business

MARCELO ADOLFO GENGOSA

DISCLAIMER

The purpose of this book is to give you some of the best kept secret strategies of top internet network marketers that I've discovered and learned to sponsor more downlines. Please note that the use of this guide is no guarantee that you will achieve the results and earnings mentioned or implied in this guide. It is not intended to give advice on investment, income guarantee or any product or services nor is any representation made that any products or services referred to or discussed on this book are suitable for any particular person.

Every precaution has been taken to ensure that the information in this guide is correct and complete, and no liability is assumed for any errors or omissions, real or perceived. The author reserves the right to update or edit this book in accordance with new conditions at any time.

The author and all other persons associated with this book expressly disclaim liability for errors or omissions in such information. Neither the author nor any other person associated with this book may be held liable or responsible for any kind of loss or damage that may result from the use of the contents of this book or to acts or omissions made by any person on the basis of the contents of this book.

NOTE: You have the permission to print one copy of this book for your own use. You may copy the pdf file for the ebook to a back-up drive or cd for your own file back-up use.

THANK YOU FOR CHOOSING TO BE ETHICAL and for maintaining the integrity and quality of the information provided within this e-book.

This training e-book is meant to be used for information and educational purposes by the reader. So have fun while using it in your network marking business to survive and become successful in your Internet Marketing Business.

COPYRIGHT INFORMATION

CONTENTS

INTRODUCTION

How to survive and become successful in your Internet Network Marketing and Home Based Business.

Dear fellow network marketer and home based business owner,

Welcome to Sponsored More Downlines. One reason I wrote this training book is because I want to share with you the experiences and lessons learned in my network marketing and internet marketing career, and hopefully it helps you in doing your business successfully.

In this book, I'll give you some of the best kept secret strategies of top internet network marketers that I've discovered and learned.

I'll give you some of the best kept secret strategies of top internet network marketers that I've discovered and learned.

I'll give you an outline of the exact formula I use to build successful internet network marketing and home based business using the internet and new tools with internet technologies.

These strategies that I am going to share with you are very helpful in order for you to generate 10-50 leads (or qualified prospects) daily and can recruit up to 10 direct downlines per week, as long as I do not force my friends, relatives, and acquaintances convince them for my business, nor do I give flyers to people I know in the streets.

I will provide you with EXACT strategies that you will learn how to leverage and power the Internet so you can create qualified prospects continuously and eventually sponsor them in your network marketing business or convert them into customers.

Do you know that you are advantage than your competitors because of the new skills and strategies you will learn in this training book that 99% of all networkers do not know yet.

We have many things to say but all of us are focusing on the reality that our industry has grown significantly since the internet has come. The old and traditional ways of MLM and network marketing prospecting are not as effective as ever, and most of them are already obsolete. Most traditional tactics are just tiresome, activities that are not productive and cannot give a clear result.

But the good news in this book is to have many new ideas to learn that you can apply your network marketing or home-based business. Ideas that you can help make you a successful in your business.

If you try to promote your business in a traditional way but do not work for you, don't worry, because there are new and effective ways and strategies to build your MLM business more faster in our generation today.

You can also start with networking, and it's better to do so by introducing you to effective strategies that you can apply and use immediately.

Here's good news... The strategies I teach you will be much easier and more enjoyable compared to the traditional way of building a MLM business where we were taught to invite and treat nicely our relatives, Friends and acquaintances who are often not interested in the MLM business you are in.

If you're like me, you'll probably also be able to give away flyers on the road and make fun of people you do not know for your opportunity.

If you're doing these things, just a friendly advice, But stop it. Because base on my experiences and the many network marketers that have been talking with and friends, these cheap strategies are no longer effective.

Marcelo Adolfo Gengosa

One of the reasons why many do not want networking is because of prospecting methods' too. They do not want to do such things.

WHY USE THE POWER OF INTER-NET FOR YOUR BUSINESS?

Here's what you think is good, It's a great time for us today because of the Internet. Your prospects are now here to find you in:

Facebook, Google, YouTube, Yahoo, Instagram, Tweeter etc ...

Your prospects are spreading all over the internet, every day they are logged in to Facebook, they are on google to research and they are in YouTube to watch videos. Here are the reasons why you would like to learn how to use the Internet correctly for your business.

Some Interesting Facts about the Internet:

- 90% of Companies use internet and social media for advertising

- Adults spend most of their hours per day on the internet

- The average online viewer watches 12.5 hours of Online Video each month.

- An average user spends more than 5 hours a day on Facebook

- As of 2018 .... Philippines is the Number 5 Country with largest number of Facebook users in the world (Over 49 Million active users).

There are many misconceptions that it is not possible to build an MLM Business using the Internet. Because they said MLM was based on the relationship and it was impossible to build a relationship with the internet.

But here you think ... The Internet is used mainly for:

1. Researching for Information

2. Communicating with one Another

Most do not understand that internet is just a tool you can use (for free) to make it faster to communicate and to build relationships with each other.

Here's the fact my friend, in our day now, if you do not use the Internet to build your network marketing business (or if you do not use it right away) is a great chance to waste your money.

Many Networkers have been outdated now because they do not have the advantage of using the Internet for their business. Others, they use the Internet but in the wrong way.

Congratulations! Because once you've reach these part of my book, you'll have a good foundation on how to use the internet in your business right.

3 BIGGEST LIMITATIONS OF NET-WORK MARKETERS

Let's start ... First of all, I want to talk about ...

"3 Biggest Limitations Of Network Marketers Who Are Still Using Old and Traditional MLM Tactics"

These are limitations to the reason why Networkers have NEVER been successful in their networking business.

Perhaps you are wondering what the traditional way is?

If you are still asking your relatives and friends convince them to join your business, you are doing the traditional way.

If you're dishonest or distributing flyers and talking to those you do not know and offering them packages to your business, you are doing traditional way.

Think of it again, how good is the strategy that you convince your friends and relatives and pursuing the target of total strangers to work with your network marketing business?

Limitation # 1: **Unqualified & Untargeted Prospects** - Let's take the fact that most of your relatives, friends and acquaintances are not interested in starting their own business. They may be happy with their situation. They may be playing safe and do not want to take a risk to invest. Or maybe they just did not really see the opportunity of our industry.

It's not your fault that they have not seen what you have seen in the Networking industry.

It is not your fault that your acquaintances are unqualified prospects.

They are unqualified because none of them comes to you and asks about your business or about the product you are selling.

The time you offer them your products and opportunities, 99% of the time you are convincing people who are not interested in whatever you offer.

In marketing principle, offering something to people who did not show any interest for your product or opportunity ... is a HUGE mistake.

Limitation # 2: Lack of Prospects - I do not know how many people you know but in fact, the number of relative and friends you know is not enough on to build a large downline organization.

Many networkers have quit since they have run out of prospects. They may have offered all the people in their warm market and they are no longer able to offer their opportunity so they decide to quit.

Limitations # 3: Lack of Funds - Most of the Up-lines will not tell you this, but I think you'll need to know why, so I'll tell you now... If you have the traditional way to use it to build an MLM business, you'll need a long journey. This means that you will have a continuous budget for your hustle, grind and funds in raising your network marketing business.

Just guess what about your taxi or bus fare, prospect meet up in Starbucks, in fast food, your house gatherings presentation and other expenses. The expenses you buy clear books, flyers, stickers, trainings fees, monthly maintenance. Uh!... (you are just started).

During training Awareness, the Trainor does not tell you about these that you need to have a continuous budget for your own to market your products and services to make your business expand. I think it's good for you to know that not just you're only paying the membership as an investment in your business.

So many Networkers are burned-out because they run out of money to fund and support the growth of their business they run out of fund (No Action).

The 3 limitations are the reason why 97% of networkers are struggling with their MLM business.

In this book, I'll give you an idea on how you can solve your problems and limitations.

I will teach you how to have 10-50 "Qualified" prospects everyday even at home with your cell phone, computer or laptop, and using the INTERNET.

When did you have last 30 prospects for a day. Day by day you can have an autopilot prospecting and even if you are just in the comfort of your own home (or while you are traveling)?

And when you're able to apply the ideas that I'm going to teach you, you'll never convince and force your prospects again, because this time. You're the one will be contacted with your prospects! You will learn how to become a Magnetic Networker!

Do you want to learn how you can do it?

Before all, there is an important concept behind ALL of what I will teach you. You need to know and understand this concept. This is absolutely CRITICAL to your success in this industry.

This concept is called... "CLOUDYOU MARKETING"

What is a CloudYou Marketing? It is basically a strategy where you position yourself on the internet as a value giver and leader (rather than a salesman with no other word but to sell and promote) for you to be able to attract the right people to you, and build trust and fast relationship with your target prospects.

For most networkers, teaching their way to build their business is to convince and offer their friends, family and acquaintances to their opportunity.

And since the number of their warm market is limited, they are forced to approach total street strangers, in the mall, in the park or anywhere. The majority are forced to do prospect kidnapping and distribute flyers.

Serious question ... Do you think that these strategies are effective for you to find your life long business partners?

Do you think that these are the "Professional" way of doing network marketing? Are you happy to do all these? Be honest with yourself. You know it's NOT-WORKING (Not Networking).

The biggest problem of 95% of networkers is how to get the qualified prospects that they offer in their opportunities or products.

The solution to this problem... LEARN INTERNET MARKETING!

If you have proper marketing skills, you can generate unlimited numbers of qualified prospects using the internet.

And it's not just prospects ... But qualified prospects, those who are prospects interested in what you offered with the opportunity are all about.

Marketing is simply positioning what you have to offer in front of the people who are interested and looking for it.

If you really want to use and take advantage of the Power of the Internet for your business and If you want to be able to attract qualified prospects to you. You may need to have your own website or your "own online shopping store". (Hep... hep..hep ...). Do not panic because it's not difficult and it's not expensive to have your own website, there are still free ones.

A type of website that is most effective to use is a type of website called "Funnel". The Funnel is a type of website where you can publish content such as blog articles, videos, or even audios in a step-by-step process.

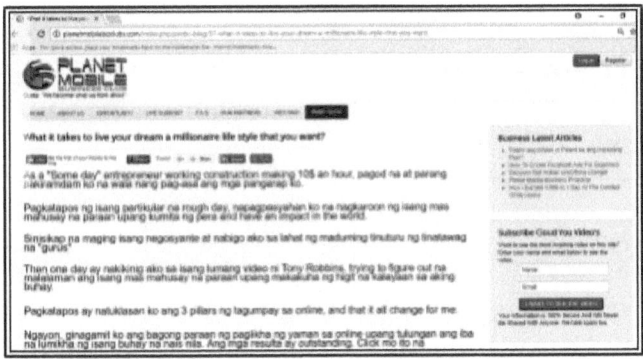

Fig.1 Example of Websites (Blog)

In your Funnel, you'll also be able to capture contact information of prospects visiting your website. You can do so through the so-called Lead Capture Form (LCF).

Fig.2 Example of Lead Capture Form

There is only one purpose of LCF placed on your Funnel Landing Page ... To capture the contact information of the prospect visiting your website.

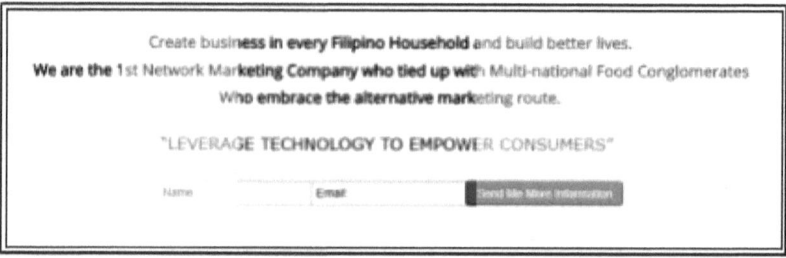

Fig.3 Example of Lead Capture Form

You will be able to capture the contact info of your site's visitors if you offer something valuable (that is relevant to your products or opportunity that you are offering) in exchange for their information like free newsletter, free training, Free E-book, free video training, etc ...

For Example:

If you are selling grocery products, the types of prospects that are best for your products are people who want to save expenses from monthly grocery. When someone visits your website, you can offer something valuable like a free E-book that the topic is "How to save your monthly expenses on grocery items".

Only interested people will be willing to give their contact information to request a copy of your E-book. This makes them a qualified prospect and they are the ones who will be interested in the products you sell.

And since they provide you with contact information, you also have the permission to contact and follow up them, they are part of your list of subscribers.

With your Funnel and lead capture form, you'll be able to generate highly qualified prospects to interact with whatever your email list are. Successful and Intelligent network marketers and home business winners use that strategy to get the endless supply of interested prospects.

Just try to imagine if you have only 10 to 50 qualified prospects interested in your offer you can contact and talk to them every day. Your advantage is vast compared to most networkers who are struggling to find at least one prospect per day.

A Funnel is also a great way to position your-self as a leader and an expert. You can achieve that by posting valuable and helpful articles. You will be able to self-identify a person who can KNOW, LIKE and TRUST.

I still want to make you more aware of why it's important to have your own Funnel or Website and why you cannot rely to use the company provided website that you have today.

WHY IT'S IMPORTANT TO HAVE YOUR OWN FUNNEL OR WEBSITE ?

1. Most Company Websites are focus on Products and Company background only, they are Online Brochures. Your prospects are looking for "solutions" for their problems. Simply showing them pictures of bottle of food supplement and telling them how stable and who's the owner of your company is not going to solve their problems.

2. All members of your company are using the same company replicated website you are using. In order to be attractive to your prospects, you may want to stand out with your competitors. Yes you are competing with your crosslines. You need to separate yourself from the mass majority.

Be Unique!

Do you think how unique if the website you are using is also used by hundreds of thousands of people? There is nothing...

Having your own website is a great way for you to become unique and be perceived as a leader and expert.

3. Most company websites are not designed to capture your prospects contact information because they are usually designed by "web designers" and not marketers.

If It's a good design website, that's good if we're going to talk about it, but we're not doing business with a website, we're here to get it right for marketing opportunities.

And even if your company website collects contact info, you are not in control of the information that your prospects are going to received.

Most networkers have no idea here on the concepts and strategies I teach you. And when you've already applied this knowledge, you're going to have a very BIG advantage than over 95% of other network marketer and home business owners out there.

In CloudYou Marketing I will teach you step by step on how to set up your Funnel website for your own so you stand from the crowd and attract prospect to you. I will also teach you how to set up your Funnel lead capture form so you can start generating high quality and interested prospect for your business. Click here to learn more about CloudYou Marketing

Now, let's talk about how you can deal with your prospects and how you can do it yourself that your prospect will volunteer to join you.

The topic is very important and I want you to understand the concept of it. There are some networkers who have heard this concept but most of them do not get it or they do not understand it.

Imagine what happens to your business if someone calls, texts, or emails you because they want to join your team and want to do what you do.

Would you like to learn how to do that? If your answer is yes, what you can do and learn is

CLOUDYOU MARKETING

One reason why a prospect is willing to join you is, if you are a person with VALUE to offer them. If you are a type of person and with all the knowledge to teach them to be successful.

CloudYou Marketing is becoming the person who has tremendous value to offer and have the information and solutions that can help others for them to achieve success.

Basically, the first thing you can do to make your value increase with your prospects is to Educate Yourself.

You can learn about Effective Marketing Skills, Generating Leads, etc... And because you are started this training, you begin to increase your value. Congratulation again!

You can also buy courses or you can find mentors who teach you to make your value increase faster. Then apply the new knowledge you learned and offer what you learned to people who are looking and in need of what you already know (apply and teach what you learn).

In this way you become a solution provider and that's why they will be attracted to you.

Read very carefully the quote below, it can change your business building approach forever.

> *"Nobody who bought a drill actually wanted a drill, they wanted a hole, therefore, if you want to sell drills, you should advertise information about making holes - NOT information about drills" ... Perry Marshall*

What does this mean? Is that making sense? As networkers our products and opportunities are not what you and I really think they are. People do not care about our product and opportunity. Not really!

No one joins the Network Marketing because he/she just wants to be networker or because he/she wants to start a business. Nobody buy food supplement because he/she just wants to take a food supplement.

That is why they join or buy the business package is because of the solution that your product and opportunity can give them, so they can solve their problems. Your job, is to position yourself, your product and your opportunity as the solution to their problem.

Here is the problem with the MLM industry, most networkers are ... "We have the best company, we have the best products, we have the best marketing plan, we are the best team, blah, blah, blah..."

And the teaching of the majority is hustle, hustle, hustle..., invite, invite, invite... Or recruit, recruit, recruit...

Do you think you're offering a solution when you do that? Do you think it is attractive to your prospects? Do you think they will see you expert and leader if you convince and forced them for your opportunity?

Your prospects are out there looking for solutions to their problems and someone who can provide that solution.

Be the Solution Provider!

Offer people real value and offer them solutions. Maybe you'll ask me how to be Valuable or how to be an Expert not even earning yet or you are just getting started!

I myself say that you have value that can be offered with other people even if you are not earning any money. Even if you are just a beginner. Even if you're not yet together with the top 10 income earners in your company. Your value is not connected with Money.

You are Valuable and you are capable of helping others!

Do you know how valuable you are in your life? It's simple just to tell other people the wrong decisions that you make and instantly you becoming valuable to others because they're going to learn from your mistakes.

And when you start attracting people to you and your website and they start becoming your prospects, you can have lots of sales and sponsored more downlines to recruit. And the more you market your business the right way, the MORE money you'll make!

YOUR INTERNET MARKETING BEST FRIEND

E-mail Autoresponder

This time, I'll introduce you to your new best friend ... Let me introduce you to your new online Best Friend ... Autoresponder!

The autoresponder is a software and tool that you can use to make you able to communicate with hundreds, thousands, and even a hundred thousand people, with just a few mouse clicks or in AUTOPILOT!

Do you start to get interest with your best friend's?

Here are some of the autoresponder's capabilities for you and your business. After your prospects have started, you can set up sequence of follow up emails using an autoresponder and you can schedule Follow up these emails to send daily, every other day, once a week, twice a week. It's up to you.

In this way can keep communicating with your prospects and you can continuously build relationships with them in autopilot.

Autoresponder is very important for your MLM and internet business. Just imagine if you start generating 20, 50, 100, 500 or 1,000 prospects.

You will not be able to follow up with them individually. If you have a problem, with Autoresponder, it can handle unlimited number of subscribers and unlimited number of messages and send them in autopilot instantly.

With the help of your best friend Autoresponder.

- You can build huge list of high quality prospects.

- Build relationship with your prospects

- Send your offer, presentations, updates.

- Sell products.

- Recruit new downlines

An AUTOPILOT while you sleep, while eating, or while you're playing with your kids. That's how powerful is with this technology. This is true Leverage.

There are number of trusted autoresponder services out there. And you usually pay a monthly subscription to use their services. Usually $30 up to $50 per month. What I use and the most affordable of all is the company called "AcyMailing" and you can buy this good for 1 time life time.

One time a blog subscriber emailed me and asked ... "Is **CloudYou Marketing coaching effective**?" Here is my reply to him ... "Only if you study it, understood it and TAKE ACTION".

My point to him is this, there's no sense of learning internet marketing and CloudYou Marketing if you do not apply what you learned.

I hope you take action now because I'm going to be honest with you, if there is no action and if you do not apply those that I share with you it is useless. Whatever the strategy teaches right knowledge is worthless because your action will give you the result.

DRIVING TRAFFIC

After you've set up a Funnel and your lead capture form, your next challenge is how you can get people who visit your blog. This is called Website Traffic. I'm so excited because this is what we're talking about in these topics.

We will talk about the so-called **Traffic Generation**. There are so many strategies to get traffic to your website. There are also paid strategies and also free.

When paid strategy, obviously there is money you will be spending. The only advantage of a paid strategy is that you can easily drive too many traffic to your website in just a couple of minutes.

When you have free strategy, there is no cost but you have to spend time and effort before you can drive a lot of traffic. It's up to you to decide which method is for you. My tip is focus on free strategy first (If you're starting to internet marketing) And slowly study paid strategy as you progress.

Today, there are two Free Traffic generation strategies I will teach you. You need to pay attention because this is what you are going to do to get prospects on your website or Funnel blog. (Just a few of the many free strategy methods I know on how to market online!)

TRAFFIC GENERATION STRATEGIES

1. Forum Marketing - Forums are places where people meet and go with similar interests. There are different types of forums available. There are forums for hobbies, for sports, for business minded, and there are also dedicated for Networkers.

First thing you need to do is to sign up for a free account in these forums. The most important thing to remember is that, you will not go or join a forum to promote or advertise your business opportunity and products. So you have to add value to other members and to put your own leadership in place.

In these forums, you'll be having a signature file. Signature file is a link attached and will be located at the bottom of all posts you make in that forum.

Once people notice you because of the value you share on these forums, they will start to be curious about you and a way to find out who you are and what other offer you have, they will click your link in your signature file.

In your signature file, the best link you can put is the blog link or your squeeze page.

2. Blogging - Creating blog post and small articles that will interest your target market is another good way to attain traffic and high search engine placings for your blog. In blogging, it is also important to provide value to your readers; you can make blog posts about tips, advice, strategies or even reviews. Then you can share the link of your post in your Facebook wall or in forums where you are a member.

This is a great way to funnel traffic back to your blog. Just do not forget to give value and give peoples enough reason to click your link to visit your blog or website.

Your blog can be the "Funnel" to your sales page or opt-in form where you direct your prospects to your business or products presentation. Remember, that here I have shared with you are just a bit of knowledge and strategies on how to use internet business.

And I want to teach you more, there are tons of ways to get more prospects to visit your Funnel or website but these 2 strategies are good to get you started.

In CloudYou Marketing I will teach you all the traffic generation strategy that I am using in my business so that you can also start sending interested prospects in your own websites or blog.

Now, I want to share with you the fundamentals of List Building. Seriously, these are one of the Crucial Elements of Online Network Marketing. Because the topic is not only very important, it is because the whole point of Internet is the most comprehensive Internet Networking and Online Marketing is BUILDING YOUR LIST.

ALL successful Internet Networkers, Online Marketers, even Motivational Speakers I know have a huge database of their followers, customers or prospects. That is their List.

If you have to remember everything I teach you here is that ... The money IS in the List! There is no reason why you do not have your own list.

Building your own personal database of targeted prospects is the entire goal of what we're doing here ... And your Blog and Lead Capture Page will help you build your own list.

I give you an Idea why the list is important... When you offer your prospect your business opportunity, it may not be the right time for them to join you even if they are interested.

They can even don't have money, they can even still be busy, etc., They may also doing their present opportunities. But because they are in your LIST and you are able to communicate and build relationships with them anytime, you can introduce them again the opportunity when the time comes for them.

I hope you understand the importance of building your own list because as a marketer, the list is your real Business asset.

Remember you can build relationship and you can follow up with your list in complete autopilot with the help of your auto-responder.

Quick Recap

Let's put together all our learnings, of what again should you do if you want to use technology and the internet to build your business. Let's put it in a Step by Step manner.

Step 1: Set up your Funnel blog with a Lead Capture Form in place. It is very important to have a way to capture people's information so you can follow up with them in the future.

Step 2: Is setting up your Automated Follow Up System. Set up your autoresponder. This part is where you're starting to learn how to leverage technology by using automation. Create at least 10 follow up messages to follow up with your prospects. You can sequence your follow up campaigns to send every day or every other day, it's up to you.

Step 3: Begin your marketing strategies, I taught you two very powerful marketing strategies which are "forum marketing" and "blogging". Start participating in forums like storya.net, Entrepreneur.com and other forums. But not here yet are your learnings ending up discovering with other powerful marketing strategies, you are just started. Continue on learning new marketing strategies.

Step 4: Start creating your content. Read other blogs about network marketing and internet marketing start learning and then share what you've learned in your blog. Do not forget to be yourself in your blog, share your personal experiences and your own story to your readers. Share your background, your passion, the reason why you are doing MLM, etc. Sharing your own story is also a way to make yourself more popular because your story is well, Unique!

Step 5: Continue on building relationship with your subscribers and followers by sending follow up message, notify them if you have new articles, new blog posts, etc. Keep a consistent communication with them and you'll nourish your relationship with your followers.

Always remember that your main goal is to build relationship to your list so they will know you more, like you and trust you. When they know, like and trust you, they will buy from you and they will join you.

Network marketing will always be a relationship business; internet and technology are the tools that can help you connect with people in a much faster and much easier way.

Take action on what I have shared with you. Your success will be your result and what you can do for your life is very well worth the effort to master the strategies I teach you.

HOW TO SUCCEED FAST

I am sure that today you have a deeper foundation and understanding about Internet Marketing.

If you reach in these parts and till now, I want to reach your hand because I want to acknowledge your willingness to learn. I know you're the type of person really committed to become successful in Network Marketing.

I will be honest with you, learning Internet Marketing and **CloudYou Marketing** will not be simple and too easy just like walking in the park or just eating a piece of cake.

These is not a get rich quick scheme. This is REAL and Powerful Strategy. You can have many new skills, new principles and new methods to learn. There are also times when your determination, persistence and commitment will be tested.

Nothing really shortcuts to be successful.

One of my advices to you is to find a Mentor or a Coach.

One of the reasons why I am quickly learning internet marketing is because I look for people to teach and coach me. I also tried to invest in knowledge and myself.

You would rather have someone teach you what you need to do to avoid mistakes that will slow down and waste your time.

Almost all successful people have mentor or coach. Not just business, Just think of popular athletes whom you know. they achieved success with the help of their coach.

A Mentor is like a compass to you, they're going to show you the right direction. They'll be there for you as your guiding light.

I want you to visualize these in your mind.

Imagine you're standing in a room and in front of you there are three Doors. Each door has a white paint and a golden door knob.

Fig.4 Door Access

In these Three Doors, one brings you to Success and the two doors drive you to Failure.

You do not know what's the right door is for you to enter these are what you can do.

First: Just stand up and do not take action, Just wait and do not make a decision.

Many Networkers like these, they are so afraid to fail and do not want to take a risk so they do not take action.

These is called "Playing safe".

Or they are hoping for other people for their success. They are waiting and hope for the spill over from Up-line. They have been waiting that one day this downline become a monster recruiter.

It's as easy as getting hold and just waiting for what works.

Like the typical behavior of most people that nothing else did but to watch TV at night, watch the NetFlix then after will complain why they have no attainment in life. They complain about their work, hoping to increase their wages and hope to lower down the goods prices. Just cross their fingers and hope that something good happens in their lives ... (I hope you do not choose that option)

Second: Close eyes, take it easy and choose the door and pray for the jackpot. Whatever! Just bump. Maybe you'll be lucky.

Many networkers do this without knowing it. Doing something here and there, even if they are not sure whether they are productive or effective of what they are doing.

They were soldiers who started the battle with no bullets on their guns.

Distributing flyers, communicating with people they do not know, prospect kidnap and daring that there might be interest in joining them.

In other words, just try and do it as trial and error. Does trial and error work? Yes. But it works very slowly. What if you're doing trial and error later you know already that you are grandfather when you become successful, you may not enjoy the sacrifice you have done.

Third: Ask the person who is behind the door. **That's the power of having a Mentor!** It does make more sense just to ask the person behind those doors, right?

Why are you guessing, or crossing your fingers and having a lottery mentality in your MLM business while you can also find a mentor and coach to help you.

This is called leveraging other people's experience and leveraging other people's knowledge.

- A mentor **can save you from years of struggle** building your MLM by teaching you effective strategies.

- A mentor will **show you the pitfalls** of short-term strategies and, you will find out what really works and what does not.

- A mentor will tell you what you **need** to hear and NOT what you **want** to hear.

- A mentor can **monitor your progress** to make sure you are in the right track.

- A mentor can **help you avoid fatal mistakes** and make sure your work accumulates to your personal success. There is nothing more frustrating than lots of your effort wasted. Too many people work hard in MLM only to find out that they have to start over again and again.

- A mentor can **share with you his / her experiences** and you can learn a lot from it.

- While other people have paid the price of trial and error, your mentor can **give these results for free**. That will surely save you from so many frustrations.

- Mentors can **inspire you and guide you** to the right direction.

- Your mentor can **guide you through the mine fields of "Hype"** He can tell you if one person made a big check at the expense of 100 people receiving no check.

Do yourself a favor. First, decide now that you are committed to be successful, and to be successful in network marketing, you need to become a lifelong learner.

You need to educate consistently and as soon and as fast as possible, and your best option is to find a knowledgeable and reliable mentor.

I'm glad that you became a part of this Free Training book, and for me to become as your virtual mentor or online coach.

But everything has not over yet, you'll still need to continue to grow as a person and as an entrepreneur.

You know if I have the best advice to give you here, these is it... **Continue on Educating Yourself**.

All successful people and all Top Earners have one thing in common. They are all lifelong learners.

You need to continuously increase your knowledge. Increasing your knowledge will also increase your own Value. The more valuable you become, the more people will be willing to follow you.

People want to work with the people, who can really teach them, guide them how to become successful.

When you invest in increasing your knowledge, when you buy training courses and books, or when you attend training seminars, do not think about how much you spend.

Rather think of the VALUE that you can get from that investment.

The best investment you can make is to invest for yourself. Because once you've acquired necessary skills to become successful, anyone can no longer take it from those skills and nothing can stop you.

All the knowledge and new skills you will learn will be your life time assets. You can always use your knowledge often and even though when you want to.

This is your foundation where you can face any circumstances along the way in building your empire of network marketing business. Without this information you cannot move and you don't have real growth in your business. Most people success because they have ingredients blend together with a better way, strategies and understanding the so called "You can fake it until you make it" phrase.

FIVE STEPS TO GET MORE LEADS AND
SALES FROM FACEBOOK ADS

By now, most people know the amazing benefits of Facebook advertising that help scale up your business to the next level or result you want.

Facebook ads are a MUST for any internet marketing campaign strategy!

But there's a BIG DIFFERENCE between just *blindly running ads* and *mastering Facebook advertising.*

How do we tap into the massive potential of Facebook ads? Is there a step-by-step process to follow?

Yes, there is.

And that's what I'm about to reveal for the last topic we have in this book.

In previous chapters, you learn deferent Best Kept Secret Strategies, Truth & Lies, Networking Misconception, Internet Marketing Significance and on my other books "Objection Crusher" you learn how to answer Prospect Objection we talked about the 25 objection that mostly ask from deferent prospect with deferent objection.

1.) Objection #1: How Much Do You Earn / Your Income?

2.) Objection #2: Think about it first

3.) Objection #3: Do I Become Rich / How Much Can I Earn From That?

4.) Objection #4: Is It Pyramiding or Scam?

5.) Objection #5: I Do Not Deal Online. I Want to be in Person?....

25.) Objection #25: I'm Interested, Can you join on my Opportunity for a Deal?

Now that we have covered what to do, it's time to learn the **5 Steps to Facebook Ad Success**.

To be successful with Facebook advertising, it is critical to master these five steps. *Without them, a marketer is just shooting in the dark*. There is no clear picture of where they are going or what they are trying to accomplish.

These steps are the gauge by which a Facebook advertising campaign is measured. If the ads aren't performing well, go back to these five steps and make adjustments.

Five Steps to Facebook Ads Success

The five steps to Facebook advertising success are probably not what most people imagine. It is easy to think it's simply a matter of writing an ad and putting it up. *But actually, writing the ad doesn't happen until step 3!*

After all, there is no point in posting an ad if there is no clear goal about where the prospect is going or what they will do when they get there.

Facebook advertising is a PROCESS and each step is critical to that overall process. The 5 Steps to Facebook Ad Success are:

1.) Landing Page
2.) Funnel
3.) Ad
4.) Targeting
5.) Optimization

Now, let's take a look at each of these steps in detail…

STEP 1: LANDING PAGE

The landing page is the page a prospect is taken to when they click on an ad. They "land" on that page. This landing page is the next step in the funnel and it helps guide people along that funnel. In fact...

The landing page is just as important as the ad!
The landing page has to be written perfect for your niche so that it gets the attention of the prospect. It needs to get them to make a micro-commitment. The key is to convince the prospect to say "Yes."

But beware. Since a Facebook ad takes prospects to a landing page, Facebook also checks landing pages for compliance. This means all of Facebook's compliance rules must be followed when writing the landing page.

With this is mind, there are different types of landing pages...

Types of Landing Pages
The type of landing page used depends on the end goal. They are as follows:

Sales Page

The sales page is generally in the form of a written sales letter or a video sales letter. The goal behind this type of landing page is to make an offer and get the sale.

Opt-in Page

The goal behind the opt-in page is to generate leads. Prospects can opt in for a free report, newsletter, mini-eBook, or something else. The prospect doesn't have to make a financial commitment. They just have to provide their email address in exchange for the free gift.

This carries no risk. If they don't like what they see when they receive emails, they can simply unsubscribe from the list.

Online Store

People who have an online store and sell physical products will want to bring prospective customers to their store or product page. This type of landing page is eCommerce-driven.

Content

This is a great way to provide value, grow a followers, and generate leads. The landing page can be a specific blog post, article, or other form of content. Just be sure to include the opportunity to leave an email address.

Webinar Registration

A webinar is another type of sales letter—a much more <u>interactive</u> one. A Facebook ad can lead prospects to a page where they can register for a free webinar. This will capture their email address and ensure they move along the sales funnel. Plus, a webinar is a great way to develop a relationship with them. After all, they are there live with the marketer behind the brand.

STEP 2: FUNNEL

In the world of marketing and sales, the funnel is the buying process that companies lead customers through. This is a gradual process of bringing prospects toward a specific goal—which is usually buying a product or service.

This process takes time! People need to warm up to the brand. They need to warm up to the person behind the brand. *There needs to be some sort of relationship.*

The truth is that shoving offers in people's faces doesn't really work. And it never has. Instead, there has to be a clearly defined funnel.

Anyone who is launching a marketing campaign needs to know where they want the prospects to end up. What is the end goal? Where do they want to lead prospects? Where do they want to make money?

One of the biggest marketing mistakes people make is that they try to sell to COLD traffic.
They don't have a clear funnel. And it is extremely difficult to work this way. It is not easy to convince someone who doesn't know the brand or the person behind it to part with their money.

What does a sales funnel look like?

The sales funnel begins with the cold market. Again, these are the people with no brand familiarity. As they are taken through the funnel, these people warm up to the brand. It goes like this:

Cold to Lukewarm then to Warm finally to Hot
Bringing them from cold to hot takes time. The process begins by generating traffic to a landing page. This page generates leads and helps grow an email list of prospects. The marketer can then build a relationship with these leads and send them offers.

Here is an example of a basic sales funnel:

Generate Leads > Offer Low-In or FREE Product > Offer Mid-In Product > Offer High-In Product

1. Generate Leads: Offer a free report or newsletter in return for their email address.
2. Offer Low-End or FREE Product: This can be an E-book or something that doesn't cost a lot of money. This does require a lot of commitment or risk.
3. Offer Mid-End Product: The customer has begun to warm up and trust. They are ready to make a bigger purchase, a bigger commitment.
4. Offer High-End Product: At this point in the funnel, the customer has become a hot prospect. They know the brand and the person behind it. They trust implicitly. They are ready to put down serious money.

Note: Relationships are being built through this whole process as well. Rapport is gained through email communication and even social media interaction.

The key is to sketch out this sales funnel to process your leads from any source of prospect and advertising on Facebook or before any ads takes place. And now that there is clarity around the Landing Page and Funnels has been created, it is time to create your Ads to run on Facebook Marketing Strategy.

STEP 3: AD

By the time a marketer reaches this point, they know:

- Their end goal
- The type of landing page they need
- Their Funnel

These things have been developed the landing page and funnel should be ready to go. There is now context around the ad. Then it's time to write the ad itself. And this is so easy to do!

But before we get into the types of Facebook ads, let's take a moment to discuss what the ads are for.

The job of a Facebook ad is to get people to STOP SCROLLING, catch their ATTENTION, and entice them to CLICK the ad.

Just think about scrolling through Facebook. What will catch the eye? What will make someone stop and take a closer look? There are a few elements to Facebook ads that depend on the type of ad.

Types of Facebook Ads

There are different types of ads, depending on the end goal and how the marketer wants to engage the consumer. Facebook constantly updates their ad types, but here are four general categories of Facebook ads:

First: Text Ads

Text ads are just that—plain text. Nothing else. These are done in a long-text format, something like a mini sales letter. It is the same as normal Facebook post that you can see in your time line but the only deferent is a sponsored post.

And they are highly effective!

Why? *Because they don't look like an ad.* Instead, they look like content. And content is what people are looking for on Facebook.

To write an effective text ad, good copywriting skills are a must. And it is easy to learn the skill of copywriting. When writing copy, even for an ad, there is a simple 5-step formula to writing it effectively.

These steps include:

1. **Introduction**—In a Facebook ad, this is the headline. It grabs the attention and makes the person want to keep reading.
2. **Story**—This is where a relationship begins being built. Make it personal. Draw people in.
3. **Content**—Create credibility. Teach them something.
4. **Transition**—Take them to the "sale," which in the case of an ad is clicking the link.
5. **Pitch**—This is the call-to-action. Tell them what they need to do. Tell them to click the ad. At this point they should want to see what's on the other side.

These steps create a narrative the person will follow. And this narrative delivers a strong message.

Second: Story Ads

The story type of ad is similar to the text ad, but it includes an image. The image is placed within the long-text format and it is ideal when selling solutions, such as:

- Consulting services
- Coaching
- Product Information

The key here is to write the copy like you would for a text ad. And it is important that the image not make the ad look like an ad. It shouldn't look salesy—it should still look like content.

This image should make people stop and take a closer look. And the headline in the text also draws attention. Then they will read the text and be enticed to click.

Third: Image Ads

The image ad has a greater focus on the image. There is only a short piece of text to accompany it. Since the image is such a prominent part of this ad type, it is a key that it grab the attention. The image ***MUST*** get people to stop scrolling.

But remember, the image is not there to sell. That's what the text is for.

Goal of the image = stop scrolling

Goal of the text = sell the click

The image is essentially taking the place of the ad headline. It needs to be powerful. Here are the qualities of a good ad image:

- Picture of people—These work well. People like to see what other people are doing.
- Picture of a product—This is ideal for ecommerce.
- Intriguing text—Any text in the image should create intrigue. Accomplish this by asking a question. In fact, the image text should read like the subject line of a good email.

Fourth: Video Ads

The final type of Facebook ad is the video ad. These ads work really well right now. People LOVE videos because they are engaging. Plus, a video is very personal. They get to see that there is a real person behind the brand. This is great for building brand awareness and a relationship with the consumer.

There are a few key attributes of a good video ad. These include:

- Audio quality—This is critical. Make sure the audio quality is top notch. If people can't hear the audio of the video, then they won't bother clicking the link.
- Use subtitles—This is always a good idea. It makes the video more accessible.
- Thumbnail image—The whole purpose is to get the per-

son to stop scrolling. This can be accomplished with an enticing thumbnail image.

- Doesn't need to be fancy—Really. Keep it simple. It's more about what is being said than having a fancy, cinematic video.
- Content—Give something of value! Teaching something or entertain the audience.
- Hook—Make sure the video has some sort of angle. For instance, what makes the product/service great and how people would benefit from it.

Pitch—Like we discussed above, the pitch is the call-to-action. Tell people what they need to do next!

STEP 4: TARGETING

Once the ad has been created, it is time to create targeting. Targeting is nothing more than selecting the specific people who will see the ad. These are the people who will make ideal customers.

Facebook's ability to target so specifically is what *sets them apart from every other advertising platform*. The data Facebook has is mind-blowing. And this data is provided by Facebook users. It is provided through their Likes, interests, location, age, gender, relationship status and a lot more.

Facebook ads allow you to target the EXACT people you want to reach.

And in the Facebook Ad Manager is a tool called *Audience Insights*, which can help anyone find the right target market. This tool provides incredible information, including trends, about any target audience, including:
- Demographics
- Page Likes
- Location and language
- Facebook usage
- Purchase activity

This information can be gathered for everyone on Facebook, a custom audience, or the people connected to a specific Page or event.

However, Facebook offers more than just this information...

Interest-Based Targeting

With Facebook, any online marketer can target their audience based on interest. And isn't that really what people base buying decisions off of? Their interests?

THIS is where all of the information Facebook collects becomes incredibly valuable for marketers.

Marketers can target based on:

- Page likes
- Interests
- Age
- Gender
- Location
- And a lot more

This is a genuine goldmine of insight into each Facebook user's world. Insight into what makes them tick. And not only can one interest be targeted, TWO can be targeted.

Intersectional Interests is a tool Facebook offers that allows advertisers to target people who match an interest AS WELL AS another interest the advertiser defines. For example, people who like BOTH Tony Robbins AND Robert Kiyosaki can be targeted. This way, those who only like one or the other will not see the ads.

This is a great way to target people who are intensely interested in a specific niche. Just think of someone who likes both Tony Robbins and Robert Kiyosaki. That person would be very interested in the *financial side of personal development*. This is a highly targeted audience.

This type of targeting will ensure ads reach the people most likely to follow the sales that has been created. But once the ad is out there, the journey isn't over.

The best marketers know they have to make sure the ads are actually working.

STEP 5: OPTIMIZATION

Once the ad is posted, that isn't the end. Not by a long shot. The performance of the ad needs to be tracked. Is it doing well? Is it getting clicks?

Not tracking ad data = shooting blind.

Tracking the ad allows marketers to tweak the ad when necessary. Maybe the headline could be better. Maybe the image isn't right. Maybe the call-to-action could be stronger.

Tracking performance and making adjustments can drastically improve performance. The good thing? All of this is easy to do with Facebook. *Facebook Ads Manager* makes it easy to test, measure, and adjust ads. And when you have ad data, it is easy to determine ROI. This is critical for any business.

There are some metrics that absolutely **MUST** be tracked. These essential metrics include:

- Relevance Score—This is a rating from 1 to 10 that estimates how well people are responding to an ad.
- Frequency—This is the average number of times the ad was served to each person. As a general rule, this should be kept lower than 5.
- Positive Feedback

- Negative Feedback
- CTR—Click-through Rate. The higher the better. This is a good indicator of how effective an ad is.
- CPM—Cost per thousand
- CPC—Cost per click (Goal = $1)

Keep an eye on the metrics of ads and TEST. Create a duplicate ad and change one variable to test exactly what is working and what isn't. Then test another variable. This is how to optimize Facebook ads.

FACEBOOK IS THE MOST EFFECTIVE WAY TO GET IN FRONT OF PEOPLE

Facebook ads are critical to the success of any marketing campaign. The audience is so immense and the targeting is so specific that getting an ad in front of the right people is easy.

But to accomplish this, these ads must GRAB people's attention. They must stop the Facebook user from scrolling. They MUST get the consumer to click. And to do this successfully, it is important to follow the **5 Steps to Facebook Ad Success**. Here they are again:

1. **Landing Page**
2. **Funnel**
3. **Ad**
4. **Targeting**
5. **Optimization**

These **5 Steps to Facebook Ad Success** have been proven to work time and time again. They ensure that the consumer goldmine that is Facebook is easily accessible.

Now for an even deeper dive into Facebook Ads and everything digital marketing, "To Grow Your Business, You Need To Grow First As A Person By Investing in Yourself and By Educating Yourself"

The information that you read from this book has been very helpful to me and my teammates. I sincerely hope you can also use them in reaching your business success.

Thank you for Reading "this book". This book is created because these ideas and concepts are not yet will known in the MLM industry, and yet they are very powerful and can help you in building your MLM business. This is reason why I wanted to share it with you.

You can use all the information you learned to take your business to the next level. But ultimately, your ACTIONS will determine your end results.

P.S If you want to learn more and want to start developing new skills and how to use technology and the internet to build your network marketing business do visit my business page.

I hope to chat with you someday (online / offline) and let's share each other success stories. Good luck and God bless.

T his E-book is valuable part of my book title "Ordinary Grocery Consumer Millionaires". You can get a copy in Amazon.com, Berns and Nobles or in any authorized distributor worldwide. It includes "Generation Sales Page, That Sale", Sponsored More Downlines", "Network Marketing Expose", "Objection Crusher".